New Race

Teachings of H.I.M. Haile Sellassie I

New Foreword: Ras Sekou Tafari

1st Frontline Edition 2017

ISBN #: 9781683650133
Library of Congress #: 2016940731

2017 Edition Editor: Prizgar G.
Print Coordinator: Prizgar G.
Book Cover Design & Page Layout: Ras Tzaddi Wadadah II

Teachings of H.I.M.
Table of Contents

New Foreword

"Who can foresee what spark can ignite the fuse"

– Haile Sellassie 1st

We at Frontline Books are pleased to take on the glorious task assigned to us, by our beloved Rastafari brethren Junior 'Ista J' Manning to republish this incredible selection of speeches made by the I Majesty Haile Sellassie 1st. These speeches were discovered by Ista J. whilst sojourning in Malawi, Southern Africa.

The speeches were chosen by Junior Manning. They are relevant to all Africans and other down-pressed peoples globally.

Members Of A New Race is a vital and compelling collection of speeches made by Haile Sellassie 1st during the latter part of the 1950's. They are still relevant today, and can be applied practically in our day to day living reality.

We at Frontline Books salute our dear brother - Junior 'Ista J' Manning for researching and making available these speeches especially for the Rastafari nation, and for the African masses across the diaspora in general.

Who are the members of the new race?

The members of the new race are those of us who are prepared, to stand up, and strive for world peace. Members of a new race, must strive to destroy (the perils of) capitalism and its appendages, such as racism, injustice, all forms of exploitation, and sexploitation; and to remove the greatest crime of humanity i.e., poverty from the face of the earth. Members of a new race must have the courage to speak out against tyranny and totalitarianism in all forms without fear of reprisals. These are some of the elements that must embody the members of the new race.

Each one of us as human beings must acknowledge the call made by Haile Sellassie 1st for us to "become members of a new race, overcoming petty prejudice, owing our allegiance not to nations, but to our fellow men within the human community."

Let us all heed the call now, more than ever, and strive to enact it in our daily lives.

Ista J. produced a splendid and most fluid piece of work, which we must add to our library collection, to enrich future generations of freedom fighters. This book should be read and comprehended in order for it to be enacted in all spheres of existence, so a difference can be made in this ongoing Armageddon. It is also a great companion, and compliments to the book *The Wise Mind of Haile Sellassie 1st.*

Haile Sellassie 1st and Menen are satisfied.

The Struggle Continues
Ready For Liberation
Ras Sekou S. Tafari
January 2017

Let us all heed the call now, more than ever.

H.I.M. Haile Sellassie I
Speaks on Spirituality

Haile Sellassie I, King of Kings of Ethiopia

The temple of the Most High begins with the human body, which houses our life, the essence of our existence. Africans are in bondage today because they approached spirituality through religion provided by foreign invaders and conquerors. We must stop confusing religion and spiritualty. Religion is a set of rules, regulations, and rituals created by humans, which were supposed to help people to grow spiritually. Due to human imperfection religion has become corrupt, political, divisive and a tool for power struggle. Spirituality is not a theology or ideology. It is simply a way of life, pure and original as was given by the Most High of Creation. Spirituality is a network linking us to the Most High, the Universe, and each other. As the essence of our existence, it embodies out culture, true identity, nationhood, and destiny. A people without a nation and is in spiritual and physical bondage because her leaders are turning to outside forces for solutions to African problems when everything Africa needs is within her. When African righteous people come together the world will come together. This is our divine destiny.

Foreword

Miichael Ibo Cooper

"World Citizenship, the dream of lasting peace and the rule of international morality is … to be pursued …"

In these words, H.I.M. Haile Sellassie I declares that humanity has a mandate and he outlines clearly the obstacle that are in the way, while at the same time reassuring us that by our faith in the inevitable victory of good over evil we must continue the pursuit. In that regard, *"Members of a New Race"* presents more fire from the flame of truth, not any one's misconstrued version but direct utterances by H.I.M.

The present understanding of world history shows us emperors being invaders, expansionist, racist, bigots, and exploiters of empires spanning way beyond their native territories. In that regard H.I.M. as Negusa Negast is the emperor who is not imperialist and Ethiopia is the empire that is a sovereign domain resisting external aggression. People who then try to apply generalizations and stereotypes find themselves in confusion, as H.I.M cannot be seen through their misconceptions. When perceived, however, through the eyes of the seekers of truth, we find H.I.M. as the uniting force of Ethiopia, we recognize as the only ruler who, in that era of Africa's history saw the need extend his descendant outside of the continent. We See H.I.M as the only ruler who, in that era of world history saw the need for spiritual and moral guidance as the backbone for administrative duties and the only monarch to leave such a vast legacy of life's instructions for his people, at home and abroad. From this inheritance we extract and pass on to *"Members of a New Race."*

Preface

Haile Sellassie I adorned with the Solomonic Order necklace and pendants.

Greetings in the name of the Most High Jah Ras Tafari; His Imperial Majesty, Haile Sellassie I, who had inspired us to spread his teachings, *"Members of a New Race"* to the four corners of the world. This booklet is a dream come through and a vision fulfilled.

In his own words, H.I.M. Haile Sellassie I, advises that *"We must become members of a new race, overcoming petty prejudice, owing our ultimate allegiance not to nation, but to our fellow men within the human community."*

This booklet *"Members of A New Race"* is part of a mission to let all the people of the world know who Haile Sellassie I is and what he stands for.

His Imperial Majesty Haile Sellassie I reminds us that; "Throughout history it has been the inaction of those who could have acted, the indifference of those who should know better and the silence of the voices of justice when it mattered most, that has made it possible for evil to triumph."

The Ras Tafari movement has been one of the most influential movements for the last sixty years. This movement is not about religion, race, color, creed or gender. It is the advancement of humanity standing against oppression of any person by any other people or persons as well as encouraging the respect of each other. Equal rights and justice for all; Truth, rights, and peace amongst mankind.

As instruments in the hands of the Almighty, we accept responsibility to eliminate false teachings under the disguise of Ras Tafari and through his inspirations, we realized that one way to get rid of false interpretations of Ras Tafari, Haile Sellassie I is to publish his exact words and teachings, so that the reader can understand for himself or herself what Ras Tafari lives for.

This compilation of information is in tribute to all people, especially open-minded African people who are lovers of the truth, letting all know that we have a rich heritage and that there is hope in the future if we follow the teachings of Haile Sellassie I.

"The Lord gave the word; great was the company of those who proclaim it."

(Psalms 68:11)

Acknowledgement

Junior "Ista J" Manning

First of all, we say thanks to Jah Ras Tafari, H.I.M. Haile Sellassie I who made this possible. This booklet was compiled from various speeches delivered at various occasions by His Imperial Majesty Haile Sellassie I, Emperor of Ethiopia. Most of the speeches were delivered between May 1957 and December 1959, and published by the ministry of information in Addis Ababa in

1960. Thanks to Michael 'Ibo' Cooper from Clarity Productions for his encouragement, motivation, vision and assistance in making this a reality. Thanks also to Bob Morgan from Rastar Productions, and all management and staff of FM 101, Malawi. Special thanks to all the people of Malawi "the warm heart of Africa," especially Ras Sidney and Ras Lion Dread for translation on the radio, all Nyahbinghi youths of Malawi, Heather Rego, her family and Paul Kite of Cooperate Graphics for graphic lay-out and printing. Thanks Jamaica, (the training ground), Rasta Vibration production all members of The Nyabinghi Order of Jah Rastafari, Pitfour Nyahbinghi Centre, Ethiopia Africa Diaspora Union Millennium Council, Rastafari Centralization organization, and all progressive Rastafari Brethren and Sistrens who shines the light of Rastafari in the four corners of the world. Special thank to my family, Ras Kirk and family who has given their diligent support in my research. Thanks to James Homiak and the Smithsonian Institute for some inspiring photo collection.

Yours – Instrument in the Hands Of The Almighty.

~ Junior "Ista J" Manning

Introduction

Lij Tafari Makonen

H.I.M. Haile Sellassie I of Ethiopia as a child was named Tafari, meaning Creator. He was given the baptismal name Haile Sellassie I, meaning Power of the Holy Trinity of Universal

Force that rule equality, (Revelation 5), Father, Spirit, and Son in Unity, fulfilling ancient tradition. Showing exceptional leadership ability, he was given the title and responsibility of Ras (administrator of one of the provinces) while still a very young man. Ras means head of Ras Tafari, meaning head creator of the House of Judah, being the two hundred and twenty-fifth from the line of King Solomon of the ancient House of David.

On the day of his crowning as Negusa Negast (King of Kings), the second of November 1930, the Emperor used his baptismal name and was universally recognized H.I.M. Haile Sellassie I, King of Kings, Lords of Lords, Conquering Lion of the Tribe of Judah, Elect of God. The Lion of Judah born on the 23rd of July, 1892 over the zodiac sign of the lion, headed education and technical advancement in Ethiopia. He is the first honorary president of The Organization of African Unity, so appointed on the 25th of May 1963 and gave the O.A.U. its first and present headquarters in Addis Ababa. He advocates international Pan African philosophy, brotherhood of African people at home and abroad. In 1955 he granted 55 hectares of fertile land from his personal land in Southern Ethiopia at Malcoda, Shahshamane, so that the sons and daughter of African origin who were displaced by the slave trade and desired reparation could be resettled through the land lordship of the Ethiopian World Federation Inc.

He is worshiped all over the Africa and the world, because there is no better African Champion than the sovereign of the only African country that delivered hard blows to colonialism. African leaders followed his successful peacemaking activities.

He is known to and admired in the world, because many times he imposed himself on world attention, even when he was regent. For example, in 1923 he succeeded in having Ethiopia made a member of the League of Nations and in 1924 when he visited Rome, Paris, and London, as well as in 1935 he delivered prophetic speech forecasting the disaster Fascism world bring about, namely World War II.

During his leadership, he made sure he was personally involved in the implementation of things that happen in Ethiopia. Being the only head of state with a universal and Christian outlook for all humanity, the world and more so Africa, admires H.I.M. Haile Sellassie I because he is a champion of peace and international cooperation. (H.I.M. Haile Sellassie I disappeared from socialist back stabbing enemies in 1975. No one knows where he has gone…)

Africa

Haile Sellassie I & Kwame Nkrumah

For Africa is potentially rich. She has enormous deposits of raw materials, and the total extent of wealth is by no means known. Africa produces large quantities of several of the world's minerals and metals. She produces large quantities of various agricultural products such as, Palm Oil and Cocoa. African people must therefore work and cooperate together if the economic development of this continent is to be furthered.

The United Nations is living tangible testimony to the value of the cooperative efforts amongst all men, to improve their way of life and preserve peace. May The Almighty God prosper that work, and grant that it may be pursued in peace, in peace of mind and of circumstances, unhindered by the fact or the threat of war.

Ethiopia depends on you, the fruits of our educational systems, to set an example to the coming generation, through your work and the life you will lead. Ethiopia's enhanced and rapidly evolving role in world life, the growth and expansion of her national endeavors makes it imperative that you students prepare yourselves for your responsibilities by being obedient to your teachers and being responsive to authority. But the attainment of any goal is never more than a temporary achievement. A mountain top is reached and beyond on the far slope, there are new lands to expire and new peaks to scale, as each goal along life's path is reached, new vistas open before us, and new challenges are made. It is indeed an immutable law of life that man's strife can never end, that the pause in life's struggle is to slip back along the road to progress. Man is born in sorrow, and of his bow brow must he earn his bread.

Africa

Present & Future

It must be recognized too, that Africa its people, its present and future are of vital concern to everyone, no matter how far moved geographically. The American people can make a significant contribution, to guaranteeing that deep and abiding friendship exists between Africa and the United States of America. Learn more about us; learn to understand our backgrounds, our culture and traditions, our strength and our weaknesses. Learn to appreciate our desires and hopes, our problems and our fears. If we truly know one another, a solid and firm basis will exist for maintenance of the friendly relationship between the Africa people and the American people, which we are convinced; both ardently from our side.

Africa has convinced our capital city of Addis Ababa last December and laid far-reaching and realistic plans for the economic integration of the continent and cooperation in the struggles against the legacy of ignorance and poverty. Until the entire continent becomes the home of the free, and until every man and every people can, in peace, labour for the advancement and welfare of the family and home land, the ideals and objectives which we have proclaimed to the world at Accra and Addis Ababa, shall not be attained. The African people can, at this time by their close cooperation and mutual assistance, demonstrate to a world torn by political differences, ideologies, and economic rivalries, a fruitful example of unity and collaboration. Confident in the guidance and support of the Almighty, and confident as we are, that fruits of education and toil may be enjoyed by all and that the people of this continent may at least assume their rightful place in the conference of nations, we call upon all to remain steadfast and together in one continental brotherhood to labour for the liberation, the progress and the welfare of the struggling people of continent of Africa.

Haile Sellassie I & various African leaders.

Africa Continued...

The moral confusion brought about by two worlds wars had led to springing up of numerous iniquitous political ambitions, destroyed mutual trust and confidence amongst mankind, and is now in the process of utilizing the superior technical skills of man for the creation of weapons capable of annihilation this earth. This liberation of our land lets in a way of light into the whole of this continent, which is now leading to the opening of doors to the nation of Africa. Our responsibility therefore, becomes indeed great; to take the lead also in striving for the unity and strength necessary for bringing our country to the level of the more advanced nations of the world.

The Value of a flag springs from the sacrifices made to defend it, as the symbol of independence, otherwise there is no difference between a flag and a piece of cloth. That is why the flag is an eternal source of inspiration, of loyalty and the symbol of the sacred duty and obligation of a soldier; to him it is a moral sentential. This has been done because we realize that food and clothing are two fundamental necessities and we have planned it so that these enterprises would contribute to the lives of our patriots and the people of Gojjam and Begendir.

To preserve the heritage of one's honour and culture is praiseworthy, but to exceed the limits may prove detrimental. They will have also violated the wish of the Almighty that by ones toil he must earn his living. Much cannot be accomplished in the pursuit of spiritual advancement, let alone that of material gains, without the help of technology. Learn! Work! We have established community education and the quest for knowledge stops only at the grave.

Haile Sellassie I at OAU gathering.

Agriculture

A country and people that become self-sufficient by the development of agriculture can look forward with the confidence to the future.

Basic Principles

These principles which we have long cherished and for which we strive are among other collective security, peaceful, and active co-existence, noninterference in the internal affairs of other nations and peaceful settlements of all disputes among nations.

Coronation

Haile Sellassie I & Empress Menen at their coronation in Addis Ababa, Ethiopia. 1930.

We shall always remember the Silver Jubilee of our Coronation, the occasion upon which we promulgated the revised constitution of our Empire, as a momentous had historic event. The revised constitution which we then granted has within a short space of time, opened a new and notable chapter in the history of our Empire. This is a great day, and indeed a memorable one. Not merely in the annals of our beloved country, but in the political history of the entire world as well. From now on, you should all open your eyes, widen your views, and cultivate in yourselves a broader way of thinking. Such as progress might bring us to the stage where our people will have the qualifications required for directly electing their own representative and sending them to us. It is however, no less true to say that there are as many types of democracy as there are nations in the world, since the underlying spirit of each type of democracy is important to it by the nation that puts it into effect in its own individual and particular way. Democracy evolve by stages gradually. Democracy as their own affairs is not foreign to Ethiopia, the democratic spirit is not new to us. It calls for clear judgment and a clear conscience. Your constant objective must be to judge and value beforehand the advantages and disadvantages of any project and its effect on the wellbeing of our entire country. No personal feelings, no concern for the narrow advantages for the few must ever be permitted to sway your judgment. The foundation of your calling is to serve, as dedicated and faithful servants, the common interests of your country.

It is today generally acknowledged that the tremendous advances made in the field of science and knowledge in our government, have been unprecedented in the recorded history of the human race. The need for the growth and development of your knowledge in this atomic and nuclear age will become increasingly evident to you as you proceed in your work.

In this irresistible march of events, this age of science, which appears to be only the beginning of things yet to come, Ethiopia cannot afford to be left alone or lag behind. If she does lag behind, it will certainly be to her detriment. In this scientific age in which we live, when the results of progress, whether baneful or beneficial, extends in their effects to the whole mankind. We have to think broad and farsighted in terms. We would have you add to the love of knowledge and science, for only thus you partake of the spirit of the modern age and serve your country in fruitful and fitting manner.

Ethiopia jealous of her freedom and having from time immemorial resisted aggression and oppression, is prepared to defend herself against possible aggressive acts. When modern armaments are combined with the well attested spirit of heroism that flows though the bloodstream of soldierly people of Ethiopia, it shall be possible for them to reply on and be proud of their bravery.

In these times when nations are engaged in a frantic armament race, particularly when occurrences that hinders peace are seen in certain parts of the world, as for example, recently in the Middle East, each country and especially those that have expressed their willingness to assume the responsibility for maintaining world peace through the system of collective security, must of necessity do their utmost to equip themselves adequately. However, as we have stated time and time again, it is our earnest belief that the only sure way of achieving lasting peace, is to place full confidence in and to apply the principles envisaged in the charter of the United nations and in the principles of collective security, thereby progressively reducing the armaments, and to invest the amount thus saved in the fields of education and public health, so essential to the promotion of the welfare of humanity.

Communication

A nation cannot prosper unless it has overcome the problems of communications.

Without communication, agriculture cannot develop, nor can commerce or industries thrive. It is communication that relates and binds people together by ties of friendship. Our country Ethiopia whose faith in God, is the basis of her own wisdom desires only to live in peace, with enmity towards none and goodwill towards all. Our faith in the essential goodwill of mankind is deep enough to assure us that the love of people on that part of the rest of the world is equally strong and abiding.

The labour of man is in vain without divine aid. Electricity is one of the indispensable factors for industrial development, in the betterment of the standard of living of people and generally the economic progress of any nation.

Defense

We, ourselves, if we fail to make adequate preparations for defense will be held to have failed both in our responsibility to ourselves and our duty to aid in the preservation of world peace. The pages of our country's history shines with the deeds of soldiers, who in the spirit of heroism inherited from their forbearers, fought in a just cause and for the preservation of peace, as well as for those soldier's statements, who in time of peace labored for the preservation of humanity's great ideals and values.

Desire & Fortitude

Although the beginning of civilization of each country vary in time, the fundamental factor that gives impetus to each country to awaken and embark on the road to progress, to reach their present level of development, are those qualities, which are enshrined in the nature of man, namely, desire and fortitude.

Turning to the problems of our continent in general, Ethiopia as the oldest independent state of Africa, has a duty towards her brethren in this continent who are still struggling for the light of freedom and independence, to do all on her part to aid them and to spare them the hardships which she herself has known. To this end, with mutual confidence and complete co-operation, we together must build that indestructible unity of African people. It is our duty to promote mutual acquaintances between our country and others.

Divine Happiness

Our happiness today must not be based primarily on material things, or it would not be any different to animal satisfaction. Each one of you should endeavor to co-operate with us, to work selflessly for the development and prosperity of our country. Should you recognize, like us, you have been chosen to serve us. You will do your duty to God and country, lest your conscience condemns you.

Education

"But, without education a man is nothing, a promise unfulfilled, a potential unrealized."

Education may be linked to a large tree with many branches. It compares various categories of instruction and disciplines each of which, like medicine, engineering naval and military sciences, police craft and aviation which calls for specialized studies, is among the vitally important activities of a nation. The benefits of education may be viewed in two ways; the first, as mentioned in your speech, is in lifting the standards of the nation. Secondly; in the shaping of development of one's character which might reflect in the direction of both good and evil. It should be your will and desire to eschew evil always pursue good.

It is for the reason, that we have never failed to stress to our people, the need and value of education. The truly educated man is endowed with a sense of obligation to society. The potentialities of education are unlimited, the acquisition of knowledge and skills class for patient learning and hard work. But, without education a man is nothing, a promise unfulfilled, a potential unrealized.

In the hands of those whose minds are not guided by a basic concern for humanity, however, education can become a dangerous and secretive weapon.

Man's education never stops, and in a profession as complex and difficult as yours, you must strive ceaselessly to put into practice, your theoretical knowledge and to keep yourselves abreast of new technical developments.

We have long recognized that raising the general level of education in Ethiopia required the opening of many institutions of higher learning, and that we should not attain our objectives, unless this was accomplished and large numbers of our people received extensive education.

We believe that education is the hope, which shall assure the progress of our people and it is our wish to assure the spread of education among all African people as much as our own subjects.

Students are the leaders of the future and are not bounded by the past. We urge you to work hard and study in recognition of the responsibility that had been imposed on you as the pioneers of the coming generations. Let it be known, that Ethiopia holds first priority on the use of this natural wealth of hers.

Time has demonstrated that those Africans who believed that the existence of an independent Ethiopia would open the door to freedom for all Africa were not mistaken in their beliefs. The family of independent nations in Africa is today growing apace, and no power on earth can now arrest this process. It would be an irredeemable error, deserving of condemnation of both history and our nation, were we to fail to seize upon this movement towards the achievement of independence and equality for all men and to carry it successfully to its conclusion.

He who would efface the sacred work of the Almighty God, he who would abuse the mysteries of God's creation and discriminate between man and man whom God created equal, on the basis of color, race or creed, calls down upon himself disaster and ruin. Let no one forge that Africans differ from no other people in the world: they love those that love them, dislike those by whom they are disliked, and are jealous guardians of their freedom.

Second, is our unswerving devotion to the principles of Collective security. In those early days of 1935-6, when our country was subjected to the horrors of aggression, we appeared before the League of Nations to plead the cause of collective security, a plea that unfortunately fell on deaf ears. But even today, no better principles can be devised for the maintenance of the peace of the world and the peace-loving nations of the world have begun to come together under this banner.

As we have started time and again. We are firmly persuaded that the path to guaranteeing the peace of the World lies in supporting the principles of collective security, and the United Nations charter, combined with a progressive reduction of the armaments, which are being built up throughout the world. The billions of dollars which are now wasted on this futile effort could which grant benefit be diverted into the constructive channels of aid for the economic growth of under developed countries.

It is our realization that education is the tested instrument by which a people reached its civilized goal that has led us to bring you to this country, to participate in the provisions which exist for this purpose.

A good educational background will enable one to help himself and his people. The uneducated, on the other hand, spends his life under the perpetual guardianship of others, just like children in their earlier years. The cultured are able to make their own decision thus avoiding domination by others, and there is nothing on earth more precious than individual freedom and community independence.

The value of unity can be best assessed by those who are enlightened, for such persons it is not easy to destroy their oneness, because their minds are matured by education. What guarantees the greatness of a state? The unity of its people. Division into races, Tribes and Sects; does not detract from such unity.

As you advance in your education, you will come to know the benefits to be derived from unity in which you will play a useful part, both for yourselves and your fellow men. With this idea in mind, we admonish you to study with all of your might.

Love the patient more than you do yourself. Unless you strictly follow this principle you may fail to fulfill the promise made in the oath that you have just taken. May God help you keep this pledge unbroken.

Political independence, however, is but one part of the complex of problems that faces the African people in their struggles to achieve their rightful place in the world. It is a paradoxical that while Africa is potentially the richest of the continents, large numbers of her people still lead an existence that can only be regarded as substandard. A major cause for this lag in Africa's economic development has been lack of education of her peoples. Let us not be too proud to face these facts and to recognize Africa's deficiencies and defects. Let us face honestly and frankly the fact that by the standard of the modern world, the African people today are poor. Our poverty need not cover us with shame.

The average wage of the African worker compares unfavorable with other areas of the world. The average African may if fate smiles upon him, receive the minimum amount of nourishment necessary for physical survival, but rarely more. In addition, the lack of capital essential to the development of their economics and the shortage of technically qualified personnel has severely limited Africa's capacity for economic growth.

Divine Power

Place your faith and trust in the Almighty God; for without his assistance and guidance, man is but a weak and puny creature.

Law of Life

By words and deeds, we have sought our beloved people to retain the past, to cleave to its faith, to preserve its tradition, to cherish its self-respect; and to acclaim the present, to recognize its challenges, to work diligently, to attain higher levels of achievement. We believe that the past must be the foundation for the future and the achievements, which we have just recounted, must be the new avenues for further progress.

This is the law of life, for nations and individuals, the law of lasting happiness and welfare. As a leader of our beloved people, it's a law, which we gladly accept ourselves. A nation without laws is a nation without discipline. Such a nation is not worthy of that name.

Good Leadership

A good leader is devoted to his work and will willingly forego even the demands of sleep to see its accomplishments. This does not mean he is impetuous. On the other hand, he maintains the balance between emotional drive and sound thinking. The true leader is one who realized by faith, that he is an instrument in the hands of God and dedicated to be a guide and will inspire of the nobler sentiments and aspirations of the people. He will kindle interest, teach aid, correct, and inspire. Those whom he leads will cooperate with him in maintaining discipline for the good of the group. He will instruct his followers in the goals towards which to strive, and create in them a sense of mutual efforts for attaining the goal.

Learning

Learning never ceases. Your learning has begun and its death will come only when your work has proved rewarding. The education you have acquired so far, will prepare you for your future work. But in these times when day to day challenges are anticipated, you must always keep in mind, the fact that you have not ceased to learn.

Leadership

It is important, however, to remember the leadership does not mean domination. The world is always well supplied with people who wish to rule and dominate others. The true leader is of a different sort; he seeks effective activities, which has a truly beneficent purpose. He inspires others to follow in his wake and holding aloft the torch of wisdom, leads the way for society to realize its genuinely great aspirations. In every significant event in history, you will find a courageous and determined leader, an inspiring goal or objective, and the adversary who sought to foil his efforts. The leader marked out by his individual craftsmanship, his sensibility and insight, his initiative, and energy.

Leaders are people who raise the standards by which they judge themselves, and by which they are willing to be judged.

But the leadership and initiative must always come from you. Do not expect them to do more than you can do for yourself. Every labourer is a father, his labour is his child. Choose your project carefully, and achieve it worthily.

We would like again to emphasize the value of time and urge you to dedicate yourself to hard work and profitable utilize your time.

There is no energy in the world including that of the atom that cannot be controlled. However, there is no scientist on earth who can control, even for a second the flow of time. For this reason, never idle away your time, however briefly.

The long history of Ethiopia as an independent state has been one replete with annals of struggles, hardship, and self-denials in difference of her independence, territorial integrity and progress. Almighty God has called us to lead our homeland through these worldwide trials of special severity in our millennia history. Yet our beloved people never hesitated to follow our leadership and thus to ensure the preservation, strengthening and development of the broad and vital national traditions and institutions which defines and characterize the **Ethiopia of today**.

All Ethiopians are the bearers of a long rich and glorious heritage that has come down to them as the fruits of the unswerving idealism, discipline, and sacrifices of their forefathers in defense of Ethiopia's integrity. This rich heritage of achievements and our centuries-old independence stand to Ethiopia as a great support and encouragement but, far more, as an urgent challenge in these hours of swift change and evolution which no Ethiopian man, woman or child can afford to ignore. We have repeatedly stated, education is the motivating force of our national life and the major safeguard of our future.

A love of high quality, we must remember, is essential in a leader. Dependability is another requirement of a leader. To be dependable is to be willing to accept responsibility and to carry out it faithfully. A leader will always be willing to take council from his people, but will often have to act on what his own mind tells him is right. This demands that the leader has trained himself out of any inordinate fear of making mistakes.

To embark successfully on a career involving leadership, demands a courageous and determined spirit. Once a person has decided upon his life work, and is filling a vital need, what he then needs is faith and integrity, coupled with a courageous spirit that, no longer preferring himself to the fulfillment of his task, he may address himself to the problems he must solve in order to be effective. One mark of the great leader is that he feels sufficiently secure to devote his thoughts and attention to the wellbeing of his subordinates and the perfection of his task, rather than being constantly worried about the approval or disapproval of others.

He who would be leader must pay the price in self-discipline and moral restraint. This entails the correction and improvement of personal character, the checking of passions and desires, and an exemplary moral character, the check of passions and desires, and an exemplary control of one's bodily needs and drives.

Leaders have to submit themselves to a strict self-discipline and develop a more exemplarily moral character than is expected of others. To be the first in place, one must be first in merit as well. It should not surprise us then, to find that the greater number of acknowledged leaders have been people who trained themselves in the art of discipline and obedience. He, who has not learned to render prompt and willing service to others, will find it difficult to win and keep the good will and cooperation of his subordinates.

Further, a leader must possess initiative, which is the creative ability to think in new ways and do new things. The leader has to always stay ahead. He cannot afford to set up procedure and then fold his hands and linger lazily watching it work. He cannot be content merely to see new trends and take advantage of them. He must keep his imagination vividly alive, so as to originate ideas and start trends.

A word of warning is in order here. To help one's subordinates or dependents at the cost of harm to the public is tantamount to sacrilege and blasphemy. It is unfortunate, that many in position of leadership both great and small, have been found guilty of such practice.

Also the spiritual training of youth. Later in the same year we laid stress on the twofold duty of education. "To teach the subjects of the curriculum, and at the same time to teach right conduct."

Ethiopia & Education

Since Ethiopia has been blessed with the heavenly grace of being a fully independent nation, and only the lack of adequate education has hindered us from profiting from circumstances and advantages of this blessing. We have personally devoted most of our efforts towards the development and expansion of education in our country, giving it priority over all our duties.

Ethiopians Satisfying Material Needs

We have been promoted to refer briefly to history of civilization, because it is our constant endeavor that all Ethiopians, in their attempt to satisfy other materials needs, to invigorate their energies, eradicate idleness and generate an unceasing desire for better and more things, shall elevate their standard of living to that of the people inhabiting other parts if the world and be able to spare others.

When we compare our country with others, we can say the forest, the rivers, the mountains and the plains constitute wealth. We should all be proud of these fortunate blessings, with which Almighty God has endowed our country.

Ethiopian Women

This is not the first time the Ethiopian Woman have served their country and their Emperor side by side with their men-folk, as history can vouchsafe this well-known fact. We are satisfied with the ability that Ethiopian women have shown in our new educational progress. Not only is our desire that in the future, women should not have less chance than men, but it is also our intention to encourage them to make equal contributions by participating with their men-folk in various projects for the development of their country. Nothing gives us greater happiness than having founded development programs and seeing that men and women are now equally benefiting from the projects which we initiated for all Ethiopia.

Example

By your efforts to understand one another, to express your sincere if divergent options, to study the viewpoints of others and attain closer cooperation in a spirit of mutual respect you are setting a fine example.

Loyalty

Loyalty being as praise-worthy as it is, you should strive to maintain it as a principle.

His teaching must be designed to develop boys and girls into loyal citizens who will respect and cherish their tradition and culture. Learning without moral education is respect and cherish their tradition and culture. Learning without moral education is fruitless and students must be taught that the true measure of value is not material advantage. In acquiring modern education, the student is not to neglect his won tradition and culture, but must to the contrary, respect and preserve all that is good in the Ethiopian way of life.

A man of any profession must remain faithful to his calling and must sacrifice his selfish interests for the sake of those whom he serves.

In this modern day when material gold and selfish aims dominate the scene of human effort, this high professional ideal of self-sacrifice and selfless devotion to one's fellowmen may appear too remote, it demands too severe. But is not meant to live for himself alone. He exists with others and for others, and it is this sense of social consciousness which distinguishes him from all other beings. And this goal can and will be attained by those who realize the tremendous potential of spiritual strength and their stay in striving ceaselessly for the attainment of this high objective.

Ethiopia has never been in her history and never will be in the future, the tool of foreign powers, and she is working resolutely and assiduously to ensue her legitimate place in the community of nations. We would firmly deal with those who would attempt to stand in the way of her progress. To overcome such attempts, an Ethiopian must always be truly Ethiopian, both in words and deeds. The greatness of nations depends upon such a spirit. We shall spare no effort in building up a future of Our people, which is consistent with Our nation's great heritage.

"To maintain one's personal freedom in honor demands self-sacrifice, which in turn, calls for valor and loyalty. We commend devotion in duty so that by your glorious military exploits, you could preserve the honor and freedom of your country."

No gift will gratify the man, who is untrue to this noble cause, serves for riches alone. The love of money can determine a man's price. So beware of the trap.

"God's word is an unfair and a bridge that leads to harmony and peace. Those that you have attired here on this occasion of the end of your abstinence we feel are profound and full of love."

The tide which is sweeping Africa today cannot be stayed. No powers on earth are great enough to half or reverse the trend. It's March as relentless and inexorable as the passage of time. The day is long overdue for a change and inexorable as the passage of time. The day is long overdue for a change of attitude on the part of those nations which have heretofore sought to hinder on impede this movement or which have been content in the past to remain passive in the face of impassioned cries for freedom, for justice, for the right to stand with their fellowmen as equals, which have gone up from this continent. It is time for them to enlist their sympathetic efforts on behalf of the struggle of the African peoples to gain the place in the world which is their God-given birthright. Those who fail or refuse to do so, those who lack foresight to realize that Africa is emerging into a new era, that Africans will no longer be denied the rights which are inalienable theirs, will not alter or reverse the course of history, but will only suffer the inevitable consequences of their refusal to accept reality.

Love

Knowledge paves the way to love, and love in return fosters understanding and leads one along the path of great common achievement for one's country.

Obedience

The words "*learn to obey that you learn to command*" must be engraved on your hearts. Unless no one is faithful no one can trust him.

Police

The responsibility of a policeman entails trustworthiness and fortitude.

Personal View of Ethiopia

We ourselves in our lifetime have labored unceasingly for the creation of the conditions essentially prerequisite to the establishment of an enduring peace. We take great pleasure in the knowledge that of our country; Ethiopia has become a symbol of hope and freedom to our brethren in all the African countries.

Spiritual Education

Specialization tends towards diversification and division among human beings; spiritual and cultural education leads them back into unity, on the national as well of the personal level.

Ethiopia, with her vast fertile lands, can compete with those nations, which have attained higher degrees of prosperity through the development of their agriculture.

Substantial Value To Mankind

This humanitarian and charitable task of helping the ailing and infirm, of keeping men and women in good health that they may properly fulfill their civic duties, is indeed a sacred duty of substantial value to mankind, going beyond all national barriers, beyond all narrow affinities of race and religion.

We can hardly think of a better means to secure mutual understanding and cultural cooperation among the people of the world, than to labour selflessly and lovingly in the field of medical service for the relief of those who stand in great need of such aid.

Teaching Profession

The teaching profession is a noble one, and we can all learn much and profit from the example set by their devoted and unselfish efforts.

Thriftiness

One should realize that thriftiness is the basis for the accumulation of wealth and economic growth of a nation. One seldom minimizes the value of money earned by the sweat of the brow however small it may be, but for the extravagant, even a huge amount of money is worthless. Know how to use your money wisely and effectively. A habit once formed becomes an incurable second nature. Therefore, utilize your wealth for worthwhile things and avoid employing it for the harmful purpose and for momentary pleasures. What are the things you possess? What was your objective in acquiring them? Use your savings where it pays you most. The hoarding of money does not yield dividends! If you wish your savings pay you higher dividends, join it with those of your fellow citizens. It is through hard work, know-how and patience that you will be able to increase your capital.

Man Proposes, God Disposes

Ethiopia, jealous of her freedom, has always had to struggle, both for the sake of her territorial integrity and for the preservation of her religious liberty. The heroism developed in the blood of our people and passed from generation to generation had served to this day as a bulwark of our freedom, so that the *Ethiopia has never had to bear the yoke of slavery. To this, history and the world bear witness*.

The glories and advantages of freedom cannot be purchased with all the world's material wealth. Freedom's price is the sacrifice of the lives; of innumerable heros and in deep realization of this, it becomes the duty of free men everywhere to be ever prepared for the defense of their freedom.

The purpose of the organization is in essence, the securing of the highest attainable standard of health, to every human being 'without distinction of race, religion, and political belief, economic or social position." In her long and glorious history, Ethiopia has time and again, had to struggle against overwhelming odds, to preserve intact her traditional freedom and independence, and to guarantee that from generation to generation the right of free men, to work out their destines without interference or hindrance. The world is only now coming to realize that Ethiopia and

Africa have long recognized, that peace, independence and the prosperity of mankind can be achieved and assured only by the collective and united efforts of free men who are prepared to maintain eternal vigilance and labour unceasingly to protect these precious of Gods' gift.

Technical and scientific advances have combined to raise mankind to a level of material achievement never before realized.

We are particularly gratified and proud that this development has been so marked and widespread on the great continent of Africa. Africa will no longer be 'The Unknown Continent,' for its human and material resources are beyond measure, and this great continent now stands on the verge of an economic, political, and cultural development which, when realized, will be without parallel in history.

As an integral part of Africa, Ethiopia looks back with pride to the role, which she has played in the history of Africa's development. With other great and free nations assembled toady in Ghana, Ethiopia contemplates the future of Africa with confidence

Mankind today had reached a level of material achievements never realized in the world's history, and it is an important mission of the independent African states to insure that these benefits are guaranteed to all people of Africa and to eliminate poverty, backwardness and illiteracy from the African continent.

History of modern Ethiopia, combining as it does, profess in modernity with antiquity of tradition. Ethiopia has been especially blessed with an abundance of natural resources and the prolific amount of her annual rainfall makes her aptly to be called "The Water Tower of the Horn of Africa." Millions of square miles of territory together with millions of human beings and their livestock depend on the water that flows from Ethiopia's mountains, and from her comes more than two thirds of the water of the Nile.

It is the duty and privilege of this generation and prosperity to conserve and develop these precious resources. To fail to do so, will be to fail in our God given responsibilities.

We express our most profound gratitude to God Almighty for having inspired us to envisage this project, and having enabled us to see it inaugurated. This is not to say money is not essential for meeting your needs, and those of your families. However, one must be so overcome by the desire for riches that he neglects the greater and nobler aim.

Man & Technology

Today, while man remain incapable of controlling his insatiable lust for power and wealth, and persist in using force as a means of satisfying his desire, his ability to wreak destruction on his fellow men is steadily increasing. Technology and science have produced in abundance the weapons whereby human life can be wiped off the face of the Earth.

Mutual Trust & Confidence

The foundation and essential characteristics of healthy society are mutual trust and confidence. Unless man undertakes the improvement of his society in co-operation with others, his striving for wealth becomes mere wishes. Do not be the victim of temporary contentment and petty satisfaction. Aspire for worthwhile aims that shall be ideals of succeeding generations. The fruits of one's sweat and mental labor are always rewarding, not only to one's self, but also his succeeding generations. Be resolute in your work and attempt to complete whatever you undertake; if you face failure, try again and persist in your determination to attain your aim. Develop a healthy pursuit of life, and do not limit your efforts to satisfying your self desires.

Nurses

This said, it become necessary for us to repeat to you today, the words of advice which we gave in 1956, to your sister nurses, on the occasion when they similarly received at our hands, their certificates of graduation: "Your profession calls discipline, the discipline of studies and devotion to obedience and duty, and the discipline of life-long devotion to learning, since knowledge knows no bounds."

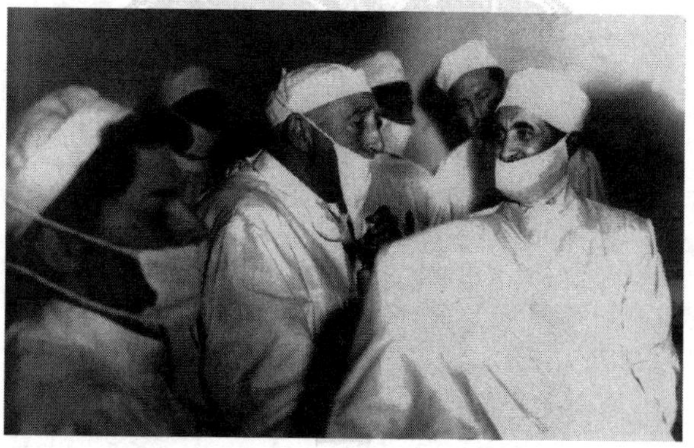

His Imperial Majesty Haile Sellassie I Speaks On Positive Mental Attitudes

"We must caution you that lasting progress can be built only on deep and enduring foundations: a strong and visible economy; example programs dedicated to the public welfare; the application of modern science and technology to the solution of some of the problems which face us and the improvement of the way of life of our people, but these in turn require an increasingly mature, rational and responsible attitude of mind and spirit, manifested in the approach which we take the exercise of our rights and obligations, in the manner in which we search for solutions to the problems of our daily lives, and in the way in which we arrange our relations with our fellow men.

It's this mental attitude, which is most essential. If our nation is to continue to prosper and develop, we must become increasingly self-critical, increasingly willing to analyze the efforts, to experiment, to admit our failures as we take pride in our successes.

We must draw on what is valuable and meaningful in our history and tradition and merging this with the best in modern learning. If the foundations, which we lay today, are not sound and strong, they will surely crumble tomorrow, and the future development of the nation will be endangered and our efforts, however well intentioned, will have gone for naught.

But it is all too easy to forget that the rights carry with them obligations that we must equally prepare to discharge the correlative responsibilities, which lay upon us.

No one has the right to education unless he is prepared to use his learning properly, in the service of his nation and fellow men. No one possessing power can claim any absolute right to exercise it unless he does so rationally and responsibly, in full recognition of procedures and requirements, which hedge around its possession and use.

No one is vested with any inalienable rights to liberty or property, who does not equally admit that these rights are limited and restricted by the reciprocal exercise by others of their identical rights. No one has the right to act arbitrarily or irrationally, or without having given the fullest consideration to the consequence of his action. No one can claim his proper measure of self-respect who does not exercise his rights and discharge his obligations in full consciousness of the rights of others.

Examine your own work and that of your fellows willingly and critically — but in a constructive rather than a destructive sense. Ask before you criticize, whether you yourself possess the defect you decry in others. Determine to profit by one another's knowledge and experience for learning from those who already know is in itself educated. Seek out the facts; aid and abet those perusing the truth as well as intellectual honesty, that modern Ethiopian be well and truly created.

We ask that our people strive not only in the pursuit of their individual ambitions, but with a common and a united spirit, for the public welfare.

Unity

We have declared on various occasions, that the lack of unity is harmful to a country and of benefit to others. This you have understood.

World Peace

In this age when man through his knowledge of science has created dangerous weapons to destroy himself, the responsibility of the great powers of the maintenance of world peace is well known to everyone, we believe that the exchange of visits by statesmen to talk over matters helps remove the misunderstandings and mistrust prevailing among states. One of our aims of our visit to friendly countries was implemented and strengthen this belief of ours.

Youths Must Be Productive

In particular, our youths must be steadfast and take advantage of the benefits of modern civilization. Do not fall prey to idleness, for it shall be a curse to you and to succeeding generations. You must set yourselves up as examples of determination and hard work. Plan your time and use both your physical and mental powers purposefully and productively

We must remember that man's achievements in the field of; wireless communications, aviation, medical sciences and many others have been accomplished through the ages by patience and hard work, diligence, perseverance and tenacity. It is in the light of these that we urge our youth to struggle constantly and unceasingly to achieving their aims.

Convinced that capital and labour are necessary ingredients for wealth and prosperity and that these two factors are absolute essentials for the economic development of our country, and believing that our beloved people shall apply itself to the task of its economic progress.

We have acquired loans from friendly countries. Ethiopians have courage and brace yourselves. Unless you improve your lot by the sweat of your brow, nobody will shoulder your responsibilities.

We would like you to recognize that unity is in itself strength, from cooperative systems and work in unity with your fellow men for the benefit of the common good. Therefore, we exhort you to follow the guidance of your creator; not to waiver from the goals which we have designed for your progress and wellbeing and to labour diligently for the early realization of the goal.

Facts About H.I.M. Haile Sellassie I

- Ras Tafari Makonnen was crowned Haile Sellassie I, King of Kings and Lord of Lords, Conquering Lion of the Tribe of Judah. Elect of God, on November 2nd, 1930 at St. George's Cathedral, Addis Ababa.
- The first Ethiopian Emperor to write a constitution and put it into function from his own initiative {1931}.

- The 225th direct descendants of King Solomon & Queen Makeda to sit on the throne of David.
- Haile Sellassie I was awarded the best dressed king in the world 3 times.
- Haile Sellassie I was the first Ethiopian Emperor to travel the globe.
- Haile Sellassie I coined the phrase "Collective Security."
- Haile Sellassie I caused a decree to be passed to abolish slavery in Ethiopia on March 31st 1924.
- Haile Sellassie I lead his country to victory in the war against Mussolini and his fascist army in 1935-1941
- Haile Sellassie I is totally against Nuclear Weapons.
- Haile Sellassie I in 1928 assumed title of Negus.
- Haile Sellassie I stood for all that was in education, reform, and progress.
- Haile Sellassie I is head of the Nyabinghi order.
- Haile Sellassie I kept his psyche in perfect order.
- Haile Sellassie I brought the first cars to Ethiopia.
- Haile Sellassie I brought the first airplane from Europe in the 1920's for Ethiopia.
- Haile Sellassie I introduced electricity into Ethiopia, first in the palace and in the buildings of Addis Ababa.

- Haile Sellassie I performed the function of Supreme Judge in a specially constructed building next to main palace. Standing on a platform His Highness would hear the cause as it was presented by the counsel and pronounce his verdict. This was according to the procedure established 3000 years ago by the Israelite King Solomon of whom his most exacted Majesty is a direct descendant.

- The most ancient lineage in the world is that of Ethiopia's royal family. It is said to be older than that of King George VI by 6130 years. Haile Sellassie I ruler of Ethiopia traces his ancestry to King Solomon and the Queen of Sheba and beyond that to Cush 6280 B.C.

- At the anniversary of the signing of the O.A.U. May 25th 1964, H.I.M. Haile Sellassie I uttered saying "As we renew our views that all Africa shall be free, let us resolve that all wounds shall be healed and past scars forgotten. On the subject of religious government policy is ostensible guide by Haile Sellassie I inspired statement, *Religion is personal and the state is for all*. What can we do for you, is the question invariably addressed to those who gained Haile Sellassie I attention?

- In the art of managing people, the essence of power, Haile Sellassie was proved a master of geniuses.

- Haile Sellassie I is neither forbearing or vindictive and rarely showed signs of anger. Though he never forgets, Haile Sellassie I is inclined to forgive and to exact gratitude.
- Haile Sellassie I is a lover of sports. From the laying of the foundation stone of Haile Sellassie I stadium, he quotes, “If health fails, teaching, knowledge, life itself, all comes to naught. It is indispensable, so have nothing to do with alcohol and avoid all things against which conscience speaks.”

H.I.M. Haile Sellassie I Speaks Pt.1

Interview with Oraiana Fallaci published in The Chicago Tribune, June 24, 1973.

Q: There is a question your Majesty, that has been troubling since I saw the poor running after your car and fighting over an eighteen pence dollar. What do you feel Your Majesty, when you distribute aims (charitable relief or donations) to your people. What are your feelings when faced with their poverty?

H.I.M.: Rich and poor have always existed. Why? Because there are those who work and those who don't. Those who prefer to earn their living and those that prefer to do nothing. Those that work, that want to work, are not poor. For it is true that our Lord, our Creator sends us into the world as equals. It is also true that when one is born one is neither rich nor poor, according to one's deserts.

Yes, we too are aware that distributing aims serves no useful purpose. For there is only one means to solve the poverty problem — work.

Q: Your Majesty, I'd like make sure I've understood you right. Do you mean, your Majesty, whosoever is poor deserves to be.

H.I.M.: We have said that whosoever doesn't work because he doesn't want to is poor. We have said that those who don't work starve and now we say that the capacity to earn depends on the individual. Each individual is responsible for the misfortunes, his fate. It is wrong to expect help to fall from about as a gift. Wealth has to be deserved! Work is one of the commandments of our Lord the Creator. Alms vous avez?

Q: Your Majesty, what do you think of the now disconnected generation? I mean the students rioting in the Universities, especially in Addis Ababa and…

H.I.M.: Young people will be young people. You cannot change the uncouth manners of the youth. Besides, there is nothing new in that. There is never anything new under the Sun. Examine the past, you'll see that disobedience of the youth has accrued all through history. The young don't know what they want. They can't know it because they lack experience, they lack wisdom. It is for the head of state to show the young which path to tread and punish them. When they revolt authority, it is up to us.

H.I.M. Haile Sellassie I Speaks Pt.2

Ethiopia has existed for 3000 years, in fact it existed ever since man first appeared on the Earth.

But, not all the young are wicked and only the most irreducible culprits must be punished unendingly. The others must be reduced to reason and then be persuaded to serve their country. That's how it must be.

Q: Your speech at the League Of nations, and the day you fight too. Your Majesty?

H.I.M.: Yes, indeed. Well do we remember that speech, the fascist newsmen insulted us, the words we utter to claim justice. Today it is happening to us, tomorrow it will happen to you …"

That's exactly what happened, We, also remember thc day we departed into exile because it was the most painful day of our life. Maybe the least understood too. Because it took a lot of courage. Sometimes things that do not appear inspired by courage demands great courage.

The fact is, we had nothing left except the hope of returning to govern our people. But the hope was great and as we roamed further it became a certainty. Oh, we would never had left if we had feared we might have to stay in Europe for good. We had understood how the future was shaping and nobody ever saw our despair during those years.

Q: Your Majesty, tell me more about yourself. They say you are fond of animals and children may I ask if you are equally fond of human being?

H.I.M.: Well it's hard to feel indulgent to human beings. It's much easier to show indulgence to animals and children. They are never wicked, never deliberate at least. Humans on the other hand, well there are good men and there are wicked, the former should be made use of, and the latter punished without attempting to understand why some are good and others wicked. Life is like theatre, one must try to understand it all at once and immediately. It is no longer amusing. Besides, we demand too much of men to be able to disrespect them.

Q: What do you demand of them Your Majesty?

H.I.M.: Dignity and courage.

Q: Give me some information on your dynasty Your Majesty?

H.I.M.: Ethiopia has existed for 3000 years. In fact, it existed ever since man first appeared on the Earth. My dynasty has ruled ever since the Queen Of Sheba met King Solomon and a son born of their union. It is a dynasty that has gone on through the centuries and will go on for centuries more.

H.I.M. Acknowledges Shadrack On A Visit To Jamaica April, 1966

H.I.M. Haile Sellassie I

(Except from the Lutheran Layman's League interview conducted at first by Dr. Aswald Haafman through interpreter Dr. Menasse Haile the Ethiopian Foreign Minister of Information and Tourism and second by Addo Meneke Essiahs the editor for medium, wave programmes at radio Voice of the Gospel of the Lutheran World Federation.)

Dr. Menasse Haile: - Your Imperial Majesty, what advice would you give to a person considering thc claims of Christ, perhaps for the first time?

H.I.M.: - I would tell a person considering the claims of Christ for the first time that, it is necessary to have faith in the Almighty, that it is necessary to have love, and that it is necessary to conduct one's self in a manner that we have been taught to do in the Bible. I would also advise him to seek secular knowledge, for the more one knows, the more he realizes the need for a prime mover, the need for a creator, the creator's good, and the need for ambition, and also peoples life upon earth. I would also tell him to learn and to think for himself, the ways he would serve the lord. With this understanding of it, he will inevitably find the way of serving his fellow men, for his faith will then be manifested by his conduct. If Christians behave in this way, if we did get ourselves to this fundamental task, then we would have a peaceful world, and we would be assured of not transgressing against the will and the commandments of God.

Dr. Manasse Haile: - Your Imperial Majesty, are there any incidents in your life which stands in your memory as times when faith in Christ sustained you?

H.I.M.: There many incidents in my life, times of trouble and difficulties…no matter what may befall a human being, he can always succeed in overcoming it in time, if he has the strength of faith and prays to God, for inevitably he comes to the assistance of those that believe in him and those that through their work, live an exemplary life. This goes not only for Christians in my view, but for all men. I think God commiserates with those that find themselves in misfortune in particular. When my country Ethiopia was invaded by alien forces several years ago, I was sustained in that period by my faith in God, and in the abiding belief that justice, though it may take time, however will ultimately prevail. If I did not have faith in the Almighty and his righteousness, and that justice will inevitably prevail, I would have lost hope, and like that then, the rest of the country could have been because I have attempted to maintain my life in him, and because the people of Ethiopia maintained their faith in the ultimate goodness of the world and the "GRAND DESIGN" the Almighty had for all men we were able to victoriously re-enter our country and rid ourselves of the evil forces. If I did not have in my heart, the love of God, I don't think I would have acted in the manner that I did. The love of God brings a sense of righteousness in a human being. It gives him comfort for the future, and assurance that right causes will ultimately prevail.

Addo Menke Essiahs: -Your Imperial Majesty, what does it seem to you that the Apostle Paul meant by the statement "Faith works by love?"

H.I.M.: What St. Paul says here is not a mistaken statement. You all know what kind of work he engaged in before his conversation. Later on after his conversation, he had faith in love and if he had not that, he would not have taught people that in his epistles. Neither love nor faith are separable from each other. An elaboration of this, is Paul's exposition in one of his epistles which speaks of love and peace. Without love, all our human efforts before the sight of God are useless. He loved us on our behalf, he was given as ransom, and it was because of love and his love for us that he accomplished the act of love.

Addo Menke Essiahs:- The Church is not merely a building. The church the fulfillment of the Christian life and its requirements. Thus as the name applies to the building, so is our heart the church which God dwells. After our blameless creator is sent to this world by his father, then the hearts of all believers became the Temple of God. The love of Christ cannot be pardoned by a series of questions and answers and man's soul cannot experience deeper enrichment as a result. We believe that man can at all times be bounded by his love and grace.

Progress Must Be Moral

H.I.M. giving a prophetic speech at the League of Nations in Geneva, Switzerland in response to Italian aggression June 30th, 1936.

H.I.M in an interview with the voice of Ethiopia, April 5, 1958

Q: There are people everywhere who hold that civilization has done more harm than food to humanity. They argue that, even though the so called modern progress has brought some physical comfort, it has done incalculable harm too and greatly weakened the spiritual values regarded so highly in former times. What they call spiritual values are those things which are usually associated with religion. In other words, the great progress made in the field of time has contributed to the weakening of the influence of religion and has deprived man of the inner calm that he so much needs for his spiritual wellbeing. What your Majesty's opinion on this?

H.I.M.: One cannot deny that in former times man's life had been one of toil and hardship. It is correct to say therefore that modern civilization and the progress of science have greatly improved man's life, and has brought comfort and ease in their trials. But Civilization can serve man both for good as well as for evil purposes. Experience shows that it has invariably brought great dividends to those who use it for good purposes, while it has always brought incalculable harm and damnation to those who use it for evil purposes.

"To make our wills obedient to good influences and to avoid evil therefore is to show the greatest wisdom. In order to follow this aim, one must be guided by religion. Progress without religion is like a life surrounded by unknown perils and can be compared to a body without a soul."

All human inventions, from the most primitive tools to the modern atomic energy can help man greatly in his peaceful endeavors. But if they are put to evil purposes, they have the capacity to wipe out the human race from the surface of the earth. It is only when the human is guided by religion and morality, that man can acquire the necessary vision to put all his ingenious inventions and contrivances to relay useful and beneficial purposes. The progress of science can be said to be harmful to religion, only in so far as it is used for evil aims and not because it claims a priority over religion, it is revelation to man.

It is important spiritual advancement must keep peace with material advancement. When this comes to be realized, man's journey towards higher and more lasting values will show more marked progress, while the evil in him recedes into the background. Knowing that the material and spiritual progress are essential to man, we must ceaselessly work for equal attainment of both. Only then shall we be able to acquire that absolute calm so necessary to our wellbeing. It is only when a people strike an even balance between scientific progress and spiritual and moral advancement that can be said to posess a holy perfect and complete personality, and not a lopsided one. The type of progress we have charted out of Ethiopia is based on these fundamental principles.

Haile Sellassie I Speaks On Survival

H.I.M. Haile Sellassie I stands on bomb dropped by the Italian military during Italian aggression against Ethiopia.

His imperial Majesty Emperor Haile Sellassie I Speaks...

We act while we can... less time run out and resort be had to less happy means. The great nations of the world would do well to remember that in the modern age, even their own fate is not wholly in their hands...

Who can foresee what spark can ignite the fuse? The stakes are identical for all of us, Life or Death! We all seek to a world in which men are freed of burdens of ignorance, poverty, hunger, and diseases. And we shall all be hard-pressed to escape the deadly reign of nuclear fallout, should catastrophe overtake us.

The problems which confronts us are unprecedented. They have no counterparts in human experiences. Men search — pursue the pages of history of solutions for precedence. But alas, there are none to be found. This then is the ultimate challenge. Where are we to look for our survival, for answers to questions which were never asked before? We must first look to the Almighty God who raised Man above animals and allowed him with intelligence and reason. We must put our faith in him that he will not desert us, or permit us to destroy mankind which he created in his image.

And we must look ourselves, into the depth of our soul. We must become bigger than we have ever been. More courageous. Greater in spirit. Ampler in outlook.

H.I.M. Haile Sellassie I on the front lines with his troops defending Ethiopia against Italian aggression.